JAMES MARTIN

THE BRITISH COLLECTION

300 classic recipes

JAMES MARTIN
THE BRITISH COLLECTION
300 classic recipes

Photographs by Jean Cazals and Simon Wheeler

Bounty Books

THE COLLECTION
by James Martin

First published in Great Britain in 2008 by Mitchell Beazley,
an imprint of Octopus Publishing Group Ltd
Reprinted 2008 (four times)

This edition published in 2008 by Bounty Books,
a division of Octopus Publishing Group Ltd,
2-4 Heron Quays, London E14 4JP
An Hachette Livre UK Company
www.octopusbooks.co.uk

The recipes in this book are taken from the following James
Martin titles: *Eating In with James Martin*, *James Martin's
Great British Dinners*, *James Martin's Easy British Food*,
James Martin's Great British Winter Cookbook and
Delicious! The Deli Cookbook.

ISBN: 978-0-753717-65-3

A CIP record for this book is available from the British Library.
Set in Helvetica Neue LT and LubalinGraph LT.
Colour reproduction in China by Sang Choy.
Printed and bound in China by Toppan Printing Company Ltd.

Commissioning Editor Rebecca Spry
Art Director Tim Foster
Project Editor Leanne Bryan
Editor Susan Fleming
Indexer Diana Lecore
Executive Art Editor Yasia Williams-Leedham
Designer Nicky Collings
Prop Stylists Isabel De Cordova, Sue Rowlands
Food Stylists Lisa Harrison, Bethany Heald,
   Katherine Ibbs, Chris Start, Karen Taylor, Linda Tubby
Photography Jean Cazals and Simon Wheeler
Production Manager Peter Hunt

contents

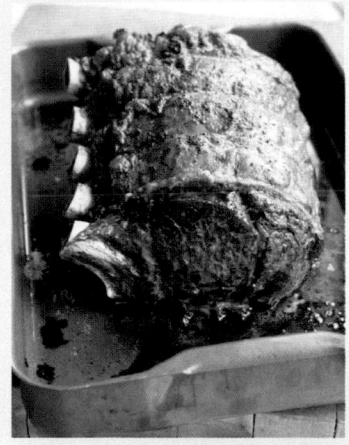

introduction

I'm probably best known for cooking British food, which isn't all that surprising, as it's been a major part of my life since I was a kid. My love of British foods developed as I watched my mum, gran and auntie cooking. Many of their dishes are included in this book, and you can't get more traditional than that.

If I grew up enjoying my gran's sponge cakes, my mum's roast beef and my grandad's poached haddock, I also grew up with dishes that we have adopted from abroad. Many of them are definitely 'British' now: I'm talking about things like kedgeree, moussaka, burgers and chicken tikka masala. They all taste fantastic, and so I've included them too.

I've also added to my collection of British dishes over the years, due to my work as a chef: through cooking at the Hotel du Vin and on the *Ocean Village* cruise ships; through speedy invention on *Ready Steady Cook* and presenting *Saturday Kitchen*; through researching British desserts for *Sweet Baby James*; and through travelling around the country meeting new people and tasting dishes for *The Great British Village Show*.

None of these recipes is difficult; in fact I've simplified the original in many cases. Although I trained as a chef, I'm not against shortcuts in cooking, and I will happily use bought stocks, ice creams and pastries. (But I've given recipes for many of these, so you can choose.)

Purist foodies may turn their noses up at some of the dishes here, but I don't care. I've been eating quiche and pizza, for instance, since my teens, and to me they're as much part of my experience of British food as apple pie and bacon butties. This book is my all-singing, all-dancing (well, I did reach the semi-finals of *Strictly Come Dancing* in 2005!) collection of foods that we celebrate in Britain, and I hope you enjoy them as much as I do.

breakfasts

I once presented a show for UK Food on asparagus and was lucky enough to visit a farm in Sussex. The season for English asparagus normally runs from May to June, for about six weeks. The most amazing thing I found at the farm was that it seemed like you could see the asparagus stalks growing; the farmer told me it was common to finish picking the field one day and then to go back to start picking the same field again almost immediately as the asparagus grows so quickly.

Asparagus Spears with Poached Egg and Tarragon Butter

SERVES 4

20–30 asparagus spears, trimmed

salt, to taste

1 tbsp white wine vinegar

4 free-range eggs

100g (3¹/₂ oz) butter

juice of 2 lemons

2 tbsp chopped fresh tarragon

4 slices brioche, toasted

Steam the asparagus over plenty of boiling water for 3–5 minutes, depending on the thickness of the spears.

Bring a pan of salted water to the boil and add the vinegar. Whisk to make a whirlpool. Once it's settled crack an egg in the middle. Simmer for 2–3 minutes, remove and keep warm. Repeat with the other eggs.

Melt the butter in a pan and stir in the lemon juice and tarragon. Pile the spears of asparagus on to each toasted brioche. Top with a poached egg and spoon on the butter sauce.

My Dad's Cheese on Toast

My father taught me this recipe – it's proper cheese on toast. This has to be one of the first culinary skills people master when they leave home!

SERVES 4

4 slices brown bread, toasted

25g (1oz) butter, softened

225g (8oz) Cheddar, grated

3 tbsp double cream

a dash of Worcestershire sauce

a dash of Tabasco sauce (optional)

salt and pepper, to taste

Preheat the grill to its highest setting.

Spread the toasts with the butter.

Put the cheese in a bowl and add the cream, Worcestershire sauce, Tabasco (if using) and seasoning. Mix well. Spoon the mixture on to the buttered toasts.

Place the toasts under the grill, and then grill until the cheese starts to bubble on the top and turn golden brown. Remove and eat immediately.

Oatcakes

I suppose the main reason why oats are thought to be Scottish is that they are the country's most successful cereal crop. There's a saying that Scottish housewives are born with a rolling pin under their arms; it's not to whack men with, but because of their love for baking. You can use finer flour for a lighter biscuit, if you like.

MAKES 16 BISCUITS

100g (3 1/2 oz) medium fine oatmeal

a pinch of salt

25g (1oz) butter, melted

3 tbsp water

plain flour, for dusting

Preheat the oven to 180°C/350°F/gas mark 4. Place the oatmeal and salt in a bowl and stir in the melted butter. Mix in enough water to create a firm, pliable dough.

Sprinkle the worktop with flour and knead the dough for a few minutes. Roll out the dough until it is about 3mm (1/8 in) thick and cut out large round cakes. On each one, mark out six to eight segments on the surface, but not right the way through. Bake in the oven for 8–10 minutes, until golden brown. Serve with any cheese you like – as long as it's British!

I'm lucky enough to have a local farmer deliver fresh eggs to me each day. But when doing my research for this book, I learned a simple thing that we take for granted – that the standard British egg has not always been British. In 1900, we imported two billion fresh eggs from as far away as Eastern Europe, so they can't have been that fresh, after all, can they?

Plain and Sweet Omelettes

SERVES 1–2

PLAIN OMELETTE

3 free-range eggs

salt and pepper, to taste

25g (1oz) unsalted butter

SWEET OMELETTE

3 free-range eggs

25g (1oz) unsalted butter

100g (3 1/2 oz) fresh raspberries

3 tbsp fresh raspberry coulis

icing sugar

Have ready a 20cm (8in) omelette pan. Beat the eggs lightly with some salt and pepper (leave out the seasoning if you're making a sweet omelette).

Heat the pan, then add the butter. When it melts, swirl it around the pan to coat the bottom. Add the eggs and shake the pan to spread them out evenly. Use a fork to draw the edges of the egg towards the centre, allowing unset egg to run to the sides. Continue until the egg is neatly set but still soft, with a little liquid on top. Take off the heat.

If you're making a sweet omelette, now add the raspberries to one half of the omelette, then flip the opposite side over it. Turn the omelette out of the pan on to a plate. Serve with the coulis and a sprinkling of icing sugar.

Yes, I know people are going to say it's an omelette Arnold Bennett, but who cares? I made this while filming in Whitby. I got the haddock from a shop called Fortune's, which is famous for smoked kippers mainly, but the haddock was brilliant. I used fresh farm eggs and cream – English, of course – and it was one of the nicest dishes I've ever made.

Smoked Haddock Omelette

SERVES 2

300ml (10fl oz) milk

3 bay leaves

2 slices onion

6 black peppercorns

280g (10oz) undyed smoked haddock fillet

6 free-range eggs

salt and pepper, to taste

20g (3/4 oz) unsalted butter

50ml (2fl oz) double cream

2 tbsp freshly grated Parmesan

Mix the milk with 300ml (10fl oz) of water, pour it into a large shallow pan and bring to the boil. Add the bay leaves, onion and peppercorns, and bring back to the boil. Add the smoked haddock, bring back to a simmer and poach for about 3–4 minutes, until the fish is cooked. Lift the fish out on to a plate and leave until cool, then break into flakes, discarding any skin and bones. Preheat the grill to high.

Whisk the eggs and season. Heat a 23–25cm (9–10in) nonstick frying pan over a medium heat, then add the butter and swirl it around to coat the base and sides of the pan. Pour in the eggs and, as they start to set, drag the back of a fork over the base of the pan, lifting up little folds of egg to allow the uncooked egg to run underneath.

When the omelette is set underneath but still moist on top, sprinkle over the flaked smoked haddock. Pour the cream over, add the Parmesan, and grill the omelette until lightly golden. Slide on to a warmed plate, and serve with a crisp green salad.

Kedgeree

My father used to cook the best kedgeree, always for breakfast. The prawns are optional, but the curry powder is a must to kick-start the flavour. A little chopped green chilli will give it the same kick if you don't have any curry powder.

SERVES 4

750ml (1 pint 6fl oz) milk

500g (1lb 2oz) undyed smoked haddock

40g (1½ oz) butter

1 onion, finely chopped

175g (6oz) long-grain rice

1 tsp medium curry powder

1 handful frozen cooked prawns, defrosted

salt and pepper, to taste

3 soft-boiled free-range eggs, shelled and quartered

2 tbsp chopped fresh flat-leaf parsley

Put the milk in a pan and bring to the boil. Add the haddock, making sure it is covered by milk, and simmer for 2 minutes. Take off the heat and allow to cool slightly. Flake the fish and pick off any bones and skin. Reserve the milk.

In a heavy-bottomed pan, melt 25g (1oz) of the butter and fry the onion for 2–3 minutes. Add the rice and curry powder, then the milk. Stir well. Bring to a gentle simmer and cook for 20–25 minutes, until the rice is cooked. Add a little more milk if it begins to dry out.

When the rice is cooked, add the haddock, then the prawns. Be careful when stirring not to break up the haddock too much. Season and put in a serving dish. Arrange the soft-boiled eggs around the edge, sprinkle with the parsley and top with the remaining butter.

Chive Blinis with Smoked Salmon and Crème Fraîche

Perhaps not so traditionally British, but this is the first dish I remember making at catering college. It is a must for any canapé tray. It's sometimes poshed up with a spoonful of caviar, but it's at its best when freshly made, and served with sliced Scottish smoked salmon and some thick, creamy crème fraîche.

SERVES 4

BLINIS

5 free-range egg whites

175g (6oz) plain flour

200ml (7fl oz) milk

1 free-range egg, beaten

1 free-range egg yolk

1 tsp bicarbonate of soda

salt and pepper, to taste

TO COOK AND SERVE

butter, for cooking

200g (7oz) smoked salmon

100g (3 1/2 oz) thick crème fraîche

**2 tbsp finely chopped
fresh chives**

Whisk the egg whites until stiff.

Mix together the remaining blini ingredients, then carefully fold the egg whites into the mixture.

Put a teaspoonful of the mixture on to a very hot, lightly buttered, heavy-bottomed frying pan and cook in a little butter for approximately 2–3 minutes on each side, until golden brown. When bubbling, flip over with a palette knife. Repeat with the remainder of the mixture.

Cut the smoked salmon into small strips. Arrange a squiggly shape of salmon on each blini and add a teaspoon of crème fraiche and a sprinkling of finely chopped chives.

I remember cooking this at college and wondering why we spent a whole day learning how to poach an egg. Now I know, as I have asked everybody I have interviewed since then to do it, and probably 50 per cent of them make a mess of it. Why? Because most of them are too busy thinking about the next fancy garnish to go on their plate, and not about what is really important. Good cooking is all about getting the basics right, and doing them well, before progressing. Delia, you are correct about that, and I thank you.

Eggs Benedict with Smoked Haddock

SERVES 4

4 x 100g (3 1/2 oz) pieces thick undyed smoked haddock fillet, cooked (*see* page 15)

1 tbsp white wine vinegar

4 free-range eggs

TO SERVE AND GARNISH

1 quantity Hollandaise Sauce (*see* page 238)

2 English muffins

a few coarsely crushed black peppercorns

a few chopped fresh chives

Make the Hollandaise sauce and keep it warm, off the heat, over a pan of warm water.

Cook the smoked haddock as described on page 15. Lift the haddock out on to a plate, peel off the skin, discard any bones and keep warm.

Bring about 5cm (2in) water to the boil in a medium-sized pan, add the vinegar and reduce it to a gentle simmer. Break the eggs into the pan one at a time, and poach for 3 minutes each.

Meanwhile, slice the muffins in half and toast them until lightly browned. Lift the poached eggs out of the water with a slotted spoon and drain briefly on kitchen paper.

To serve, place the muffin halves on to four warmed plates and top with the haddock and poached eggs. Spoon over the hollandaise sauce and garnish with a sprinkling of black pepper and chives.

Scrambled Eggs with Chilli and Crisp Streaky Bacon on Toast

Scrambled egg is so simple to make, but still people overcook it and end up with rubbery, gelatinized stuff on toast. To prevent this, add double cream halfway through the cooking while you whisk everything together in the pan.

SERVES 4

12 streaky bacon rashers

55g (2oz) unsalted butter

6 free-range medium eggs, beaten

salt and pepper, to taste

100ml (3 1/2 fl oz) double cream

TO SERVE

4 pieces sliced bread, toasted and buttered

1 green chilli, deseeded and finely diced

Heat a sauté pan on a medium heat. Add the bacon with half the butter, and cook until crisp and golden brown, a few minutes only. Remove from the pan and keep warm.

Wipe the pan and return to the heat with the remaining butter. Season the eggs well with salt and pepper, then pour into the pan. Quickly mix the eggs with a whisk and, when half-cooked, add the cream, whisking all the time.

Just as the eggs are beginning to set, remove from the heat, and season again. Spoon on to the toast, with a scattering of chopped chilli on top and bacon on the side. Serve immediately.

Gammon with Pineapple Salsa

This is an up-to-date gammon and pineapple, but do you know where I think the best gammon and pineapple can be tasted in the UK? In truckers' roadside cafés. Gammon with a grilled tinned pineapple ring, HP Sauce and chips may not be the lowest cholesterol dish in the world, but it tastes fantastic!

SERVES 4

4 slices gammon

6 pineapple rings, fresh or tinned with natural juice, chopped

juice of 2 limes

1 red chilli, deseeded and chopped

1 tbsp roughly chopped fresh mint

2 tbsp olive oil

salt and pepper, to taste

Grill or fry the slices of gammon until cooked.

Mix the remaining ingredients together for the salsa. Serve the gammon with chips, potato wedges or vegetables and a generous of serving of salsa on the side.

Smoked Bacon Welsh Rarebit

You can make loads of this cheese mixture in one go, and it can sit in the fridge for a week. Then, any time of day or night you fancy a quick snack, it's so easy to use. But serve your rarebit with the Tomato and Apple Chutney on page 370, and it becomes a very serious dish indeed.

SERVES 4–6

12 slices good streaky bacon

4–6 thin slices white bread

RAREBIT

375g (13oz) strong Cheddar

75ml (2 1/2 fl oz) milk

100ml (3 1/2 fl oz) double cream

1 free-range egg plus 1 free-range egg yolk

1/2 tbsp mustard powder

25g (1oz) plain flour

25g (1oz) fresh white breadcrumbs

a dash of Worcestershire sauce

a dash of Tabasco sauce

salt and pepper, to taste

To make the rarebit, grate the cheese into a pan with the milk and cream, and gently warm until the cheese has melted. Do not boil. Leave to cool slightly. Preheat the grill.

Add the egg and egg yolk, mustard, flour, breadcrumbs and a dash of both Worcestershire and Tabasco sauces to the cheese mixture. Season, mix well and allow to cool.

Grill the bacon until cooked, then grill the bread on one side only. Place the bread, ungrilled-side up, into an ovenproof dish, and top with the bacon. Pour the rarebit mixture over the bacon and bread, return to the grill and allow to colour.

Remove from the grill and cool a bit before serving with the Tomato and Apple Chutney on page 370.

Hot Stilton Rarebit

Rarebits or rabbits are centuries old, and were traditionally served as a savoury before or instead of a sweet. You can use leftovers from cans of beer, but don't replace the beer with milk as some recipes suggest; this ruins the taste.

SERVES 4

25g (1oz) butter

3 free-range egg yolks

1 tsp English mustard

90ml (3fl oz) ale or lager

a dash of Tabasco sauce

a dash of Worcestershire sauce

salt and pepper, to taste

225g (8oz) Stilton cheese, grated

4 slices toast

Preheat the grill to its highest setting.

Melt the butter over a low heat, then remove from the heat and cool slightly. Mix in the egg yolks, mustard, ale or lager, and the Tabasco and Worcestershire sauces. Season well with salt and pepper, and fold in the cheese.

Place on the toast (either on its own or with sliced tomatoes or flat-leaf parsley leaves underneath), and grill until brown on the top.

Sausage and Ketchup Sarnie

Shop around for good-quality sausages for this recipe; if you use cheap, poor-quality sausages your sarnie will suffer!

SERVES 2

450g (1lb) sausages

4 slices bread

TO SERVE

Ketchup (bought or homemade, *see* page 241)

Grill or fry the sausages until cooked.

Spread the ketchup on 2 slices of bread, then top each of these slices with sausages and another slice of bread.

If there were one meal I could request before I died, it would be my gran's bacon buttie. She's no longer with us, but if I could make a buttie as well as she could, I would be a very rich man.

Bacon Buttie

SERVES 2

30g (approx. 1oz) dripping

8 slices streaky smoked bacon

4 slices bread (bloomer or pain de campagne)

40g (1½ oz) butter

2 ripe tomatoes, sliced

black pepper, to taste

Warm a large pan on the stove and add the dripping. Separate the bacon and add to the pan – watch out for the fat spitting out of the pan.

While the bacon is cooking, toast the bread, either on a griddle or under the grill. When the bacon is nice and crispy, remove from the pan. Add the butter to the pan and melt.

Dip the bread into the pan and then place on to the plates and build up the sandwich with the bacon and sliced fresh tomatoes. Pour over the rest of the juices from the pan, grind over some pepper, top with the other slice of bread and serve.

I remember hating bees from the moment, when I was a kid, that my father decided it was a good idea to visit a local honey farm in the North Yorkshire moors. The heather-flavoured honey was great, but what of those mad people who, daily, had to face what seemed like certain death to collect it? Since then, I have tried to avoid going anywhere near bees again. This recipe is a tribute to all you beekeepers. Oh, and by the way, I think you're all bloody mad!

Pancakes with Honeycomb

SERVES 2–3

PANCAKES

1 large free-range egg

a pinch of salt

100g (3 1/2 oz) plain flour

300ml (10fl oz) cold milk

2 tbsp melted butter, plus extra for cooking

HONEYCOMB BUTTER

100g (3 1/2 oz) unsalted butter, softened

85g (3oz) honeycomb

2 tbsp runny honey

Make the pancakes by mixing together the egg, salt and flour and then slowly whisking in the milk. Just before cooking, mix in the melted butter.

Heat a heavy-bottomed saucepan on the stove. Add a small knob of butter and place a spoonful of the batter in the centre of the pan. Swirl the pan to coat the base with the pancake.

Place the pan back on the heat to cook the base of the pancake. Once the base is cooked, either flip the pancake over or use a palette knife to turn it, then cook the other side. Continue making pancakes until all the batter is used up. Keep the pancakes warm.

To make the honeycomb butter, place all the ingredients in a food processor and blend until smooth. This will keep in a covered container in the fridge.

Serve two to three pancakes per portion topped with a spoonful or so of the fragrant butter.

Hot cross buns are traditionally baked for Good Friday and are thought to originate from pagan times, but they are far too good to eat only at Easter. Here is a great way to use them as a nice breakfast or dessert (not forgetting, of course, the 'true' way to eat them – toasted with butter – but I don't need to tell you that!).

Blueberry Sauce for Hot Cross Buns

SERVES 2

250ml (9fl oz) milk

15g (1/2 oz) caster sugar

2 free-range eggs

a knob of butter

2 hot cross buns (bought or homemade, *see* page 363)

BLUEBERRY SAUCE

300g (10 1/2 oz) blueberries (or strawberries)

45g (a good 1 1/2 oz) caster sugar

a splash of port or orange juice

TO SERVE

honeyed cream, crème fraîche, clotted cream or ice cream

Put the milk and sugar into a bowl and, using a whisk, beat in the eggs. Leave to one side.

Prepare the blueberry sauce by mixing together all the ingredients, crushing the berries lightly to allow the juices to run.

Heat the butter in a pan. Slice the hot cross buns in half, dip into the eggy mixture, and cook in the butter for about 2 minutes on each side.

Remove the buns from the pan and place on a serving plate. Pile the blueberry sauce on top of the bottom half of each bun, top with 2 spoonfuls of cream or ice cream, then add the lid of the bun. Serve immediately.

soups

Watercress is near to my heart. I am lucky enough to live in a part of England where watercress is famous. Hampshire, in particular Alresford, is the home of the famous 'watercress line' that used to deliver freshly cut watercress from the beds up to London. Sadly, this doesn't happen any more – instead, the cress travels by road. But the line does still exist and, for a small fee, you can travel a stretch of it in the original steam train and carriage. Watercress is grown in beds fed by spring water from underground. It needs a constant flow of this water to grow, and is available most of the year.

Watercress Soup

SERVES 4–6

1 onion, sliced

2 cloves garlic, chopped

25g (1oz) butter

1.2 litres (2 pints) chicken stock

450g (1lb) Estima potatoes, peeled and diced

2 bunches watercress

freshly grated nutmeg (optional)

200ml (7fl oz) double cream

salt and pepper, to taste

bread croûtons, to garnish (optional)

In a heavy-bottomed saucepan, fry the onion and garlic in the butter until softened but not coloured.

Add the stock and potatoes and bring to the boil. Simmer for 15–20 minutes, until the potatoes are cooked.

Chop up the watercress (leaves and stalks) and add to the soup with the freshly grated nutmeg, if using.

Simmer for 2–3 minutes before blending in a food processor in batches, adding the cream as you go.

Return to the pan to heat through gently and season with salt and pepper. Garnish with bread croûtons – baked or fried – if you like.

Rich Onion Soup with Cheese Toasts

French in inspiration, but a real favourite in Britain now. The start of this recipe is most important. The knack of making a good onion soup is colouring the onions well first, as this will give flavour and a deep colour to the finished dish. No gravy browning – that's cheating!

SERVES 6

5 onions, thinly sliced

3 cloves garlic, thinly sliced

20g (3/4 oz) duck fat

300ml (10fl oz) red wine

150ml (5fl oz) fresh beef stock

50ml (2fl oz) brandy

100ml (31/2 fl oz) good balsamic vinegar

salt and pepper, to taste

10g (1/4 oz) fresh flat-leaf parsley

55g (2oz) unsalted butter

CHEESE TOASTS

8 thick slices white bread

280g (10oz) Gruyère cheese, grated

Sauté the onion and garlic in a large pan in the duck fat for about 20–30 minutes, colouring very well.

Stir before adding the red wine and stock. Bring to the boil and simmer for about 10 minutes. Add the brandy and balsamic vinegar and simmer for another 20 minutes.

Preheat the grill. Toast the bread on both sides, top with the grated cheese and place under the grill to melt.

Season the soup well with salt and pepper and add the chopped parsley. Pour into soup bowls. Top with the grilled cheese toasts and a knob of butter.

Leek, Potato and Stilton Soup

A classic soup with that most classic of all British ingredients: Stilton, the king of cheeses. Stilton has conquered the world, but is still exclusively made in seven dairies in Leicestershire, Nottinghamshire and Derbyshire. The best Stilton is made in the summer, with summer milk, which gives it a creamy yellow colour. It is usually sold at Christmas time. When buying Stilton, look for evenly distributed veins and a good contrast between the blue veins and the creamy cheese.

SERVES 4

1 chicken stock cube

600ml (1 pint) hot water

100ml (3 1/2 fl oz) white wine

1 medium leek, split, washed and thinly sliced

1 shallot, finely chopped

2 cloves garlic, finely chopped

1 large baking potato, peeled and finely chopped

125g (4 1/2 oz) strong Stilton cheese

125ml (4fl oz) double cream

salt and pepper, to taste

1 packet shop-bought croûtons

1 tbsp chopped fresh parsley

Place the stock cube, water and wine in a pan and bring to the boil. Add the leek to the pan with the shallot, garlic and potato. Cover and cook for 10 minutes.

Add the Stilton and cook for 4–5 minutes to melt the cheese. Add the cream, salt and pepper and blend.

Warm the croûtons. Serve the soup hot, sprinkled with the parsley, and offer the warmed croûtons separately.

I made this soup while filming in York. It's a nice twist to an old English favourite, almond soup. The vegetables came from a man called John Mannion, who is an old friend of the family. I remember going to his stall in York Market (and his shop nearby) as a kid with my gran and watching her squeeze all the fruit first before buying them. What's great now is that most of the market stalls are selling a mixture of new and traditional fruit and veg. I wonder what my gran would have thought of garlic and ginger grown in Yorkshire! Probably nothing, as they were never her thing, but she could make a great broccoli soup, and this is as near as I can get to it.

Broccoli and Almond Soup

SERVES 4

25g (1oz) butter

2 cloves garlic, crushed

1 large white onion, diced

225g (8oz) potato, peeled and diced

75ml (2 1/2 fl oz) white wine

700ml (1 1/4 pints) vegetable stock

2 heads broccoli, cut into small florets

150ml (5fl oz) double cream

85g (3oz) flaked almonds, toasted

2–3 sprigs fresh parsley, finely chopped

salt and pepper, to taste

Heat a large saucepan and add the butter. Once foaming, add the garlic and onion, and sweat without colouring for a few minutes. Next add the potato, white wine and stock. Bring to the boil and simmer for 5 minutes to get the potato cooking.

Add the broccoli to the pan and continue to cook for a further 6–8 minutes. Add the cream, half the almonds and all the parsley. Bring to the boil, remove from the heat and allow to cool slightly.

Blend in a food processor, then return the liquid to the pan. Bring to the boil and season with salt and pepper.

To serve, spoon the soup into bowls or mugs and top with the remaining toasted almonds. You could also add a little partly whipped double cream.

A twist on our traditional tomato soup. Roasting vegetables for soups, as I've done here and in the Butternut Squash and Lime Soup with Pine Nuts and Herb Oil on page 38, makes the soup taste even better. Serve with thick slices of crusty bread.

Roast Tomato and Cumin Soup

SERVES 6–8

1.25kg (2 3/4 lb) ripe tomatoes

6 tbsp olive oil

2 medium onions, roughly chopped

3 cloves garlic, roughly chopped

1 large fresh red chilli pepper, deseeded and chopped

2 tbsp cumin seeds, roasted and ground

500ml (18fl oz) tomato passata

salt and pepper, to taste

Preheat the oven to 170°C/325°F/gas mark 3.

Slice the tomatoes in half and place them on a large, heavy baking sheet. Sprinkle over 2 tbsp of the olive oil and roast for about 1 hour, or until the tomatoes are dehydrated and have caramelized. Remove the tomatoes from the baking sheet and set aside.

Place the onion, garlic and chilli in a large saucepan with the remaining olive oil. Cook over a low heat, stirring occasionally, until the onion is soft and translucent, about 10 minutes. Add the cumin and fry for another 5 minutes. Add the roasted tomatoes and the tomato passata and cook for 10 minutes.

Purée the mixture in a food processor or blender.

To serve, transfer the mixture back into a saucepan and reheat gently until warm. Taste and add salt and pepper as desired. Ladle into warm bowls. Serve with some charred ciabatta.

One-minute Chilled Tomato Soup
This soup takes only a minute as the ice cubes chill it instantly. I use plum tomatoes only if they are good ones. But if you are unsure about the tomatoes' quality, use a 400g tin of plum tomatoes.

SERVES 4

6 plum tomatoes, quartered

2 cloves garlic, roughly chopped

1 small red onion, roughly chopped

50ml (2fl oz) white wine

50ml (2fl oz) water

1 tsp tomato purée

5 ice cubes

1 x 15g packet fresh basil leaves

salt and pepper, to taste

olive oil

Put the tomatoes, garlic and onion in a food processor or blender. Then add the wine, water, tomato purée, ice cubes, fresh basil, lots of black pepper and a pinch of salt.

Place the lid on securely and blitz for about 30 seconds until all the ingredients are mixed together well. There may be some funny noises from the machine, but that's only the ice being ground up.

Remove and serve in chilled bowls, drizzled with a little olive oil, with some hot French bread and butter. You can garnish it further with some ripped-up fresh basil leaves, if you like.

Sweetcorn and Crab Soup
This may be taking its place in a British cookbook, but the idea came from one of the Indian chefs in my restaurant.

SERVES 6

1 large white onion

250g (9oz) potatoes, peeled

curry powder, to taste

30g (1 1/4 oz) unsalted butter

1.2 litres (2 pints) chicken stock

a handful of fresh basil leaves

300ml (10fl oz) double cream

salt and pepper, to taste

450g (1lb) frozen sweetcorn kernels

meat from 2 freshly cooked crabs

olive oil

Dice the onion and potatoes. In a large, heavy pan, sweat them with curry powder to taste in the butter until soft. Pour in the stock, stir, and bring to the boil, then simmer until the potato is tender, about 15 minutes.

Meanwhile, whizz most of the basil in a blender until finely chopped. Add 250ml (9fl oz) of the double cream and mix. Season and chill.

Add the sweetcorn to the soup, simmer for 3 minutes, then add the crabmeat and remove from the heat. Purée while still hot, then return to the pan, add the remaining cream, and simmer for 3 minutes. Season again. Spoon into bowls. Garnish with a little basil cream and olive oil and a basil leaf.

Not long ago I tried to grow squash in the garden and was amazed by all the different kinds available. The one we are most familiar with must be the common butternut, and since growing these I've become an even bigger fan. This soup is different to the norm; I roast the squash first as I think it tastes much better.

Butternut Squash and Lime Soup with Pine Nuts and Herb Oil

SERVES 6–8

1 butternut squash, about 1kg (2¹/₄lb)

2 tbsp clear honey

extra virgin olive oil

1 white onion, chopped

2 cloves garlic, chopped

150ml (5fl oz) white wine

500ml (18fl oz) chicken stock

25g (1oz) pine nuts

150ml (5fl oz) double cream

finely grated zest and juice of 3 limes

salt and pepper, to taste

50ml (2fl oz) crème fraîche

10g (¹/₄ oz) fresh basil, torn

HERB OIL

10g (¹/₄ oz) fresh basil

20g (³/₄ oz) fresh chervil

75ml (2 ¹/₂ fl oz) olive oil

Preheat the oven to 200°C/400°F/gas mark 6.

Cut the squash in half, scoop out the seeds, then peel it and dice the flesh into 2.5cm (1in) chunks. Place in a large oven tray with the honey and a little olive oil. Roast for 30–40 minutes.

Meanwhile, fry the onion and garlic in a little olive oil to soften, then add the wine and stock. Bring to the boil and simmer for 3–4 minutes.

Sauté the pine nuts in a little olive oil until golden brown. Remove and leave to one side.

To make the herb oil, chop the basil and chervil and place in a blender with the olive oil. Blend to a fine purée. Season and leave to one side.

Remove the squash from the oven and place it in a blender with the stock mixture, cream, lime juice and lime zest, and blend. Season well. Return to the pan to the heat and check the seasoning.

Pour into individual bowls, and top with a dollop of crème fraîche. Drizzle with the puréed herb oil, pine nuts and the basil. Serve.

I thought this dish up in Prince Charles's Duchy Estate in Cornwall, where I stumbled across a farm shop while filming for the BBC. It had over 30 different types of squashes! I bought a pumpkin, which I roasted when I got home and made into a great, inexpensive, vegetable soup.

Puff Pastry Crusted Pumpkin and Rosemary Soup

SERVES 6

1 small pumpkin, about 1kg (2 1/4 lb), peeled, deseeded and diced into 2.5cm (1in) chunks

1 white onion, chopped

2 cloves garlic, chopped

2 tbsp clear honey

3 fresh rosemary sprigs

extra virgin olive oil

500ml (18fl oz) chicken stock

100ml (3 1/2 fl oz) white wine

150ml (5fl oz) double cream

juice of 1 lemon

salt and pepper, to taste

TOPPING

200g (7oz) ready-rolled puff pastry

1 free-range egg yolk, beaten

Preheat the oven to 200°C/400°F/gas mark 6.

Place the pumpkin, onion and garlic in a large oven tray with the honey, rosemary sprigs and a little olive oil. Roast for 25–30 minutes, until the pumpkin is cooked and golden brown. Keep basting the pumpkin as the honey may catch on the bottom of the tray. Remove from the oven.

Heat the stock and wine on the stove. Place into a blender with the pumpkin mixture, cream and lemon juice, and blend until smooth. Check the seasoning, and keep to one side.

On a slightly floured worktop, open out the ready-rolled pastry and, either using four large ovenproof soup dishes or four smaller deep dishes, cut the pastry out into four circles, 2cm (3/4in) bigger than the rim of each dish.

Fill the dishes no more than three-quarters full with soup and brush the edges of the dishes with the beaten egg yolk. Place the pastry on top and crimp it down on to the egg to seal. Use any of the leftovers to make a small pumpkin-shaped piece on the top.

Brush the pastry with the egg and bake for 15 minutes, until golden brown on the top. Serve piping hot.

This cheap soup has great strong flavours, but go carefully; a common mistake is to use too much saffron, as it takes a while to get the right colour and flavour. The soup goes well with the caramelized onions, which I like to make loads of at a time – I also use them in sandwiches and with cheese, especially Cheddar.

Mussel and Saffron Soup with Caramelized Onions

SERVES 6

50 mussels, scrubbed and bearded (discard any that do not close when tapped)

75ml (2 1/2 fl oz) dry white wine

1 tbsp olive oil

2 tsp minced garlic

a pinch of crushed red pepper flakes

1/2 small onion, chopped

1 tsp tomato purée

200ml (7fl oz) double cream, whipped

500ml (18fl oz) fresh chicken stock

1 tsp saffron strands

1 tbsp chopped fresh chives

salt and pepper, to taste

CARAMELIZED ONIONS

2 tbsp unsalted butter

2 onions, halved and thinly sliced

Caramelize the onions first. Melt the butter in a medium sauté pan over a low heat. Add the onions and sauté until caramel brown, about 30 minutes, stirring occasionally.

To make the soup, combine the mussels and wine in a large, heavy pot over a high heat. Cover and cook, shaking the pot occasionally, until the mussels open, about 4–5 minutes. Discard any mussels that do not open. Drain, reserving the mussel liquor. Shell 40 of the mussels. Strain the reserved mussel liquor through a fine sieve.

In a large saucepan over a medium heat, heat the olive oil, and sauté the garlic and pepper flakes until the garlic is light brown. Add the chopped onion and sauté until tender, about 5 minutes. Add the reserved mussel liquor, the tomato purée, cream and stock. Bring to a boil and skim off any foam that develops.

Lower the heat, add the saffron and simmer for 5 minutes. Add the shelled mussels and the chives, and season with salt and pepper. Liquidize.

To serve, place a spoonful of caramelized onions in the centre of each bowl and scatter a few mussels around in their shells. Then pour the soup over the lot.

Pea Soup

I was brought up on this, and I love it! My gran used to put chunks of leftover ham with the bone in this soup, which adds extra flavour. I like it with fresh mint leaves thrown in at the end. But soups can be easily overcooked and none more so than this: the last thing you want is a wrinkly bullet in the bottom of your soup bowl.

SERVES 6–8

1 bunch spring or young green-stemmed onions, chopped

2 cloves garlic, chopped

25g (1oz) unsalted butter

600g (1lb 5oz) podded young peas

675g (1½ lb) leftover cooked/ boiled ham, roughly chopped

600ml (1 pint) fresh chicken stock

250ml (9fl oz) double cream (optional)

salt and pepper, to taste

1 fresh mint sprig (8–12 leaves), chopped

Sweat the onion and garlic in the butter in a covered pan for 5 minutes, without colouring.

Add the peas, ham and stock, and bring to the boil. If using the cream, add now and simmer until the peas are tender, about 10 minutes.

Season to taste, and liquidize if you like, adding another 25g (1oz) butter. But why bother blending? I think it looks and tastes so much better when you can see the bits of food you're eating (and without the extra cream). Serve sprinkled with the mint.

salads, terrines & pâtés

Salad of Chargrilled Leeks and Red Onions with Mozzarella

The thing I love most about this dish is the dressing; I sometimes serve it with plain little gem lettuce and some croûtons or, even better, warm French beans and seared tuna or salmon. You can change this salad totally by adding smoked chicken or plainly cooked chicken. You could also use a mild British cheese instead of the mozzarella.

SERVES 4

a pinch of caster sugar

salt and pepper, to taste

24 young leeks, trimmed

2 red onions, cut into wedges

2 x 200g mozzarella balls, cut into 4 slices each

DRESSING

4 tbsp tarragon vinegar

1 tsp Dijon mustard

1 tbsp chopped fresh tarragon

50ml (2 fl oz) extra virgin olive oil

1 tomato, deseeded and finely diced

1 tbsp fine capers, rinsed and drained

1 tbsp stoned green olives, finely chopped

1 hard-boiled free-range egg, shelled and finely chopped

Make the dressing first. Combine all the ingredients and leave for an hour or so for the flavours to come together.

Bring a large pan of water to the boil with the sugar and a little salt. Throw in the leeks, return to the boil and cook gently for 2–3 minutes. Drain them well and dry on a cloth.

Grill the leeks and onions on a hot, ridged cast-iron griddle pan. When they are tender and slightly blackened, remove from the heat and season with salt and pepper.

Toss the leeks and onions in most of the dressing, then divide between four plates. Arrange two slices of mozzarella over each portion, sprinkle with the remaining dressing, and serve.

Stilton and Red Onion Salad

This is another one of those dishes I did in my first year at college, and I remember it because it's so simple. So once more, it's very 1970s, I suppose, but then again I did eat it a lot in Berni Inns …. Stilton, to my mind, needs a strong robust flavour to accompany it, and red onion fits the bill for this salad.

SERVES 4 AS
A STARTER

4 red onions

2 tbsp olive oil

2 tbsp groundnut oil

2 tbsp balsamic vinegar

a squeeze of lemon juice

salt and pepper, to taste

10 very thin slices baguette

225–350g (8–12oz) mixed green leaves

115g (4oz) Stilton cheese, broken into pieces

DRESSING

3 tbsp port

2 tbsp Dijon mustard

2 tbsp red wine vinegar

4 tbsp walnut oil

4 tbsp groundnut oil

Cut each onion into six wedges, keeping the root of the onion in place to prevent it falling apart. Bring a pan of water to the simmer, add the cut onions and cook for 2 minutes.

Warm together the oils, balsamic vinegar and lemon juice. Drain the onions and add them to the oil/vinegar mix. Remove from the heat, season with some salt and pepper, and leave the onions to marinate at room temperature, turning every so often to ensure an even flavour. The onions will be at their best after an hour or so.

Preheat the oven to 200°C/400°F/gas mark 6. To make the dressing, boil and reduce the port by half and allow to cool. Mix the mustard with the red wine vinegar. Whisk together the oils and pour slowly on to the mustard and vinegar mixture, while continuing to whisk vigorously. Once all has been added, whisk in the reduced port and season with salt and pepper.

Crisp up the sliced bread by drizzling with a little extra oil and baking for 5–10 minutes.

To serve, separate the red onion wedges, and remove from the marinade. Mix with the green leaves and Stilton. Add some of the red wine/port dressing to bind. Place on a plate, trickle over some more of the dressing and sit the crispy toasts on top.

Seared Salmon with Sesame Watercress Salad

This is a modern twist to a recipe that uses two great British ingredients: salmon and watercress.

SERVES 2

2 x 200g (7oz) salmon fillets (no skin or bone), cut on a slant

olive oil

salt and pepper, to taste

50g (1 3/4 oz) watercress

2 tbsp sesame seeds, toasted

WATERCRESS DRESSING

50g (1 3/4 oz) watercress, blanched

25ml (1fl oz) rice wine vinegar

125ml (4fl oz) grapeseed oil

Make the dressing first. Blend together all the ingredients in a food processor and leave to one side for the flavours to infuse.

Heat a cast-iron griddle or frying pan on the stove until very hot and brush the salmon on both sides with a little oil. Season and then fry on both sides for 3–4 minutes.

While the fish is cooking, place the watercress on the plate and then put the cooked salmon in the middle.

Sprinkle the toasted sesame seeds over the top, drizzle with the watercress dressing and serve immediately.

This salad is great: charred aubergine (which we Brits have come to love) served warm with roast loin of lamb. I put watercress and coriander in the salad with red onions, but spring onions will work well, too. The lamb comes from the best end, which has been removed from the bone and trimmed down.

Lamb, Aubergine and Watercress Salad

1 x 600g (1lb 5oz) lamb loin, trimmed of fat and silver skin

olive oil

salt and pepper, to taste

2 small aubergines, cut into 1.5cm (5/8 in) slices

BALSAMIC VINAIGRETTE

4 tbsp balsamic vinegar

1 clove garlic, finely chopped

a pinch of caster sugar

125ml (4fl oz) olive oil

leaves from 2 fresh thyme sprigs

WATERCRESS SALAD

100g (3 1/2 oz) watercress, stems removed

25g (1oz) fresh coriander, leaves picked

1 red chilli, deseeded and cut into strips

1 red onion, halved and sliced

rind of 1/2 salted lemon or preserved lemon, cut into strips

Preheat the oven to 220°C/425°F/gas mark 7.

Brush the lamb with olive oil and season with salt and pepper. Heat a frying pan over a high heat and seal the lamb on all sides until browned. Transfer the lamb to a baking tray and roast for 6–8 minutes for medium. Set aside to rest for 5 minutes before slicing.

Preheat an overhead grill or ridged cast-iron grill to a high heat. Lightly brush the aubergine with olive oil and cook for 5–8 minutes, or until tender and browned. Keep warm.

Meanwhile, to make the balsamic vinaigrette, whisk all the ingredients together until combined. Season to taste with salt and pepper.

To make the salad, combine the watercress, coriander, chilli, onion and lemon rind. Add enough balsamic vinaigrette to moisten it.

To serve, place two to three slices of aubergine on each serving plate. Slice the lamb loin into discs, about 5mm (1/4 in) thick. Arrange the salad over the aubergine, and the lamb on top. Finish with a further light drizzle of balsamic vinaigrette.

Egg and Bacon Salad

Here is an easy salad that can be served on its own or as a starter. You can, of course, poach the eggs as a change, or use pancetta instead of streaky bacon. When doing the latter, though, crisp up the pancetta on an oven tray. This will stop the pancetta sticking to the grill tray while cooking.

SERVES 4

4 slices thick-sliced white bread, crusts removed

4 soft-boiled free-range eggs (boiled from room temperature for 5 minutes in simmering water)

6 rashers thick-sliced back or streaky bacon

4 little gem lettuces, leaves separated, rinsed and drained

salt and pepper, to taste

4 spring onions, washed and finely shredded

3 tbsp red wine vinegar

2 tbsp each of olive and groundnut oil, mixed

Cut the slices of bread into 1cm (1/2 in) dice. Shell the boiled eggs, and cut into quarters.

The bacon can now be pan-fried until crispy in a nonstick pan with no oil. Any fat content will be released into the pan from the bacon. This will also happen if grilling. Whichever method you choose, keep the bacon fat for frying the bread. Once cooked, remove the bacon from the pan and keep warm.

Add the bread dice to the bacon fat, and fry until golden and crispy. You might need a little extra oil to achieve a golden colour.

Season the salad leaves with salt and pepper. It's best, whenever making salads, to sprinkle salt around the bowl and not directly on to the leaves. This prevents the salt from falling on to wet leaves and sticking in lumps.

Chop the bacon into chunky strips, and mix into the leaves with the spring onions and fried bread. Mix together the red wine vinegar and the oils. This can be spooned over the leaves, adding just enough to coat.

Arrange in a large bowl as one large salad. The soft-boiled egg quarters can now also be seasoned with salt and pepper and placed among the leaves. Serve immediately.

Bacon and Bean Salad

The dressing is the key to this delicious salad. Its texture is a bit like that of a Caesar salad, but less creamy and heavy. It's a pain to remove the shells of broad beans, but it will be worth it. You'll need about 200g (7oz) fresh or frozen large beans to end up with 100g (3 1/2 oz) here.

SERVES 4

8 slices dry-cured streaky bacon or 10 slices Parma ham

50g (1 3/4 oz) fresh white bread, crusts removed, cubed

a knob of unsalted butter

150g (5 1/2 oz) mixed red and white chicory and rocket

100g (3 1/2 oz) cooked French beans

100g (3 1/2 oz) podded, blanched and peeled broad beans

5g (1/8 oz) fresh flat-leaf parsley, picked and washed

extra virgin olive oil

Parmesan shavings (optional)

DRESSING

2 slices white bread, crusts removed

4 tbsp milk

juice and finely grated zest of 1 lemon

2 cloves garlic

140g (5oz) fresh shelled walnuts

150ml (5fl oz) extra virgin olive oil

salt and pepper, to taste

To make the dressing, tear the bread into the blender and moisten with the milk. Add the lemon zest and juice, garlic and walnuts and blend to a paste. Add, and blend in, the olive oil and some salt and pepper to taste.

Grill the bacon or Parma ham until crisp. Fry the cubed bread in a little butter until golden brown.

Place the salad leaves and the beans into a bowl. Add the dressing and some salt and pepper and mix.

Place a portion of the salad on each plate and top with the crisp bacon, the parsley and croûtons. Drizzle with the olive oil and top with the Parmesan shavings (if using).

Good sausages are used as the base of this simple terrine. Play around with the flavours by using beef or game sausages instead of pork. I've used plum sauce, as this combines with the orange segments to give a sweet-and-sour flavour. When making terrines, don't overcook them or they will break up while being sliced.

Pork Terrine with Apricots and Pistachios

SERVES 8–12

olive oil

250g (9 oz) streaky bacon rashers

900g (2lb) or 14–15 large sausages (Lincolnshire are best)

10 fresh sage leaves, chopped

5g (1/8 oz) fresh flat-leaf parsley, chopped

100g (3 1/2 oz) dried apricots, chopped

75g (2 3/4 oz) shelled pistachio nuts, roughly chopped

salt and pepper, to taste

SALAD

2 oranges, peeled and segmented

55g (2oz) wild rocket leaves

1 large potato, peeled, cooked and diced

8 tbsp plum sauce (make your own, or buy the Chinese stuff from the supermarket)

3 tbsp olive oil

Preheat the oven to 180°C/350°F/gas mark 4. Take a terrine dish, 30–35cm (12–14in) long, 10cm (4in) wide, and 9–10cm (3 1/2 –4in) deep, and brush it with olive oil. Line the dish with streaky bacon, leaving 5–6cm (2–2 1/2 in) overlapping the edge of the terrine.

Make the filling by removing all the meat from the sausage skins (discard these). Add the sage, parsley, chopped apricots and pistachio nuts and mix well with plenty of seasoning.

Pile the meat mixture into the terrine mould and press down well. Fold over the bacon and either cover with the lid or with foil, and place in a bain-marie half-filled with hot water. Cook in the oven for 60 minutes. Remove from the oven, cover with foil, and press down with a weight. Cool, then place in the fridge.

When ready to serve, make the salad by mixing the orange segments, rocket and potato together in a bowl. Mix the plum sauce with the olive oil and season to taste.

Cut the terrine into slices and serve in the centre of the plates with the salad to one side and the dressing spooned over the top.

Yorkshire Ham Terrine with Spiced Pickle

Scott's Butchers in York is still the best place to buy Yorkshire pork products, but if you visit you have to queue. Last time I was there it was obviously pension day, as the place was like a bingo hall on a jackpot night!

SERVES 10

3 ham knuckles

4 bay leaves

6 black peppercorns

1 large onion, halved

1 medium leek, halved

1 medium carrot, halved

extra virgin olive oil

6–8 thin slices York ham, or other cooked sliced ham

2 shallots, finely chopped

1 clove garlic, chopped

salt and pepper, to taste

20g (3/4oz) fresh parsley leaves, finely chopped

a pinch of ground mixed spice

2 gelatine leaves, soaked in cold water for 5 minutes

55g (2oz) mixed salad leaves and herbs, such as chervil and wild rocket

PINEAPPLE PICKLE

1 clove garlic, crushed

1 tsp grain mustard

5 tbsp white wine vinegar

a good pinch of turmeric powder

150g (5 1/2 oz) demerara sugar

1 medium pineapple, skinned, cored and finely chopped

DRESSING

4 tbsp each of grain mustard, extra virgin olive oil and cider vinegar

Put the ham knuckles, bay leaves, peppercorns, onion, leek and carrot in a large saucepan. Cover with cold water, bring to the boil and simmer, covered, for 3 hours, until the meat is tender.

Meanwhile, grease a 20 x 8cm (8 x 3 1/4 in) terrine mould with olive oil. Line with clingfilm, then with the sliced York ham.

When the ham knuckles are nearly cooked, heat a little olive oil in a small pan and gently sweat the shallots and garlic.

Remove the cooked ham knuckles from the pan, reserving the stock, and leave to cool slightly. While warm, remove the meat in pieces from the bone. Place in a small bowl with the shallot and garlic, some salt and pepper and the parsley. Mix well, then pack into the terrine mould.

Strain the ham stock. Taste and, if it is too salty, dilute with water. Pour 500ml (18fl oz) into a pan and add the mixed spice. Warm gently and add the soaked gelatine; leave for 2–3 minutes for the gelatine to dissolve before stirring. Pour into the terrine and overlap the edges of the ham. Cover with clingfilm; the terrine needs to be quite solid and 'packed'. Put a uniform weight on the terrine to press it down (I use a brick) and leave overnight in the fridge.

To make the pickle, put all the ingredients together in a pan except for the pineapple. Simmer for 3 minutes, then add the pineapple and cook for a further 3 minutes. Put into sterilized jars (see page 368 for sterilizing instructions) and cool.

To make the mustard seed dressing, whisk all the ingredients together, then use some of it to dress the salad leaves at the last minute.

To serve, turn out the terrine and remove the clingfilm. Using a sharp knife, cut into 2cm (3/4 in) slices and place a slice in the centre of each plate. On each plate, spoon a pile of pineapple pickle, placing a few dressed leaves on, too. Grind over a little black pepper, and serve.

Chicken and Ham Terrine

This is one of the dishes I put on the menu at The Bistro on board *Ocean Village*, and I love it. But as with most terrines and pâtés, I think it should be served with fruit chutney or caramelized onions, or something else to break up the taste.

SERVES 10–12

16–20 slices streaky bacon (depending on the size of the terrine)

300g (10 1/2 oz) chicken meat, minced

300g (10 1/2 oz) shoulder of pork, minced

600ml (1 pint) double cream

1 free-range egg, beaten

100ml (3 1/2 fl oz) Armagnac

3 tbsp each of chopped fresh parsley and chives

2 tbsp chopped fresh tarragon

salt and pepper, to taste

25g (1oz) butter

2 shallots, finely chopped

300g (10 1/2 oz) chicken breast meat, cut into 5mm (1/4 in) strips

225g (8oz) sliced cooked ham

140g (5oz) chicken livers, cleaned

TO GARNISH

Pear Chutney (*see* page 370)

mixed dressed salad leaves

First, line a terrine dish measuring 28 x 16 x 6cm (11 x 6 1/2 x 2 1/2 in) with streaky bacon, allowing the slices to overlap the mould at the sides by a few centimetres.

Put the chicken and pork into a bowl, and work the mixture with a wooden spatula. Stir in the cream, egg, Armagnac and chopped herbs. Season with salt and pepper, to taste.

Heat the butter in a small saucepan and sweat the shallots for 2–3 minutes. Cool and add to the meat mixture.

Spread half the mixture over the bottom of the terrine, then make a layer with some of the sliced chicken breast, then some of the sliced ham, and fill with some of the remaining mince mixture. Continue with two or three layers of the ham, mince mixture and chicken breast, with a layer of the chicken livers running though the middle of the terrine. Finally, fold the bacon over the terrine from the sides and either cover with a lid or cover with foil.

Preheat the oven to 200°C/400°F/gas mark 6.

Place the terrine in a roasting tray, and half-fill the tray with warm water. Cook in the oven for 1 hour. Remove from the oven and place a weighted board (maximum weight 500g/1lb 2oz) on the terrine to compress it gently until it has cooled completely.

Serve in thick slices with pear chutney and dressed salad leaves.

Duck Liver Pâté

I hated liver as a kid, as most kids do. The only two dishes my grandad would cook were calf's liver and poached haddock. I used to watch him with his Brylcreemed stick-back hair as he pan-fried his slice of liver with precision. He never failed to try to get me to eat some as I ran out of the door in horror. I now know I was missing out on something great.

SERVES 14–16

1kg (2 1/4 lb) organic duck livers, left whole, but all green and thready bits removed

Cognac

2 cloves garlic, finely chopped

a handful of fresh basil leaves

salt and pepper, to taste

350g (12oz) unsalted butter

GARNISH

brown bread, sliced and toasted, or Melba toast

Pear Chutney (*see* page 370)

mixed salad leaves, dressed

Place the livers in a single layer in a heatproof dish, and scatter over some Cognac. It should not cover them, but they need to wallow in it for several hours. Turn them over so both sides absorb the alcohol. Throw the garlic, all but 2 of the basil leaves (torn and minus the stalks) and some salt and pepper into the brew just before poaching.

Gently poach the livers, turning them over after a couple of minutes, and continue to stew until they are cooked on the outside but pink within, about 3–4 minutes. Do not overcook them or you will end up with a drab, brown, crumbly result.

Tip the contents of the dish straight into your blender with 225g (8oz) of the softened butter, and whizz until smooth. Check the seasoning, then scrape into a large terrine dish and leave to cool.

Meanwhile, clarify the remaining butter. Gently melt it, and pour into another container, leaving behind all the curd-like sediment. Cool a little.

Pour the buttercup-coloured clear liquid butter over the surface of the pâté, place the reserved basil leaves in the centre, and put it into the fridge until it is set.

Using a hot knife, slice the terrine. Serve with a slice of toast, a spoonful of chutney and some dressed mixed salad leaves.

grills
& fry-ups

Rib-eye Steak with Caesar Salad

Rib-eye steak has only really become popular in Britain over the past ten years, but it is such a great piece of meat. It comes from the end of the sirloin part of the beef that the rib joint is attached to (where you get the rib joint for roasting from). I love steak and salad, and Caesar salad works particularly well in this case. The recipe for the dressing was invented by a chef I used to work with – cheers, Adam!

SERVES 4

4 rib-eye steaks, about 225g (8oz) each

salt and pepper, to taste

olive oil

CAESAR SALAD

2 cos lettuces

2 thick slices white bloomer bread, cubed

about 25g (1oz) butter

4 cloves garlic

150ml (5fl oz) white wine

4 free-range egg yolks

2 anchovy fillets

140g (5oz) Parmesan, freshly grated

300ml (10fl oz) vegetable oil

1 tbsp Dijon mustard

To start the salad, separate the lettuce leaves, and wash and dry well, then tear into chunky pieces. Place in a serving bowl. Gently cook the bread cubes in the butter in a frying pan until golden brown.

To start the Caesar dressing, peel the garlic and place in a pan with the wine. Bring to the boil and cook for about 5 minutes, until the cloves are soft. Using a hand blender, blend the wine and garlic together with the egg yolks, anchovy fillets and cheese, adding the oil slowly to stop the mix from splitting. (This shouldn't happen, as the cheese should make the mix blend together more easily.) Add the mustard and seasoning to taste.

Preheat a frying pan on the stove. Season the steaks with salt and pepper, and cook in a little olive oil. If you want medium, this should take about 3–4 minutes on both sides. Once cooked, remove the steaks from the pan and place them on the plate while you sort out the salad.

To serve, throw the bread cubes into the bowl with the lettuce, add the dressing, and mix together well. Season, place on plates alongside the steaks and munch away.

Rib-eye Steak with Herbs and Mustard served with Honeyed Oven Chips

Nothing beats sirloin steak, deep-fried onion rings, peas and jacket potatoes or chips. This is just a more up-to-date version of our classic steak and chips. It uses rib-eye steak that is now, thankfully, found in most stores and butchers.

SERVES 4

4 rib-eye steaks, about 225g (8oz) each

olive oil

salt and pepper, to taste

8 tbsp Dijon mustard

125g (4 1/2 oz) chopped herbs, such as parsley, coriander, basil, thyme and chervil

1 lemon, quartered

HONEYED OVEN CHIPS

500g (1lb 2oz) Estima potatoes, peeled

4 tbsp runny honey

1 tsp fresh thyme, chopped

1 clove garlic, chopped

4 tbsp olive oil

Preheat the oven to 200°C/400°F/gas mark 6.

For the chips, cut the potatoes into large, chip-sized pieces. Mix together the honey, thyme and garlic in a bowl. Whisk in the olive oil and use the mixture to coat the potatoes well.

Season the chips and place on a baking tray in the oven for 35–45 minutes.

Meanwhile, heat a ridged, cast-iron griddle pan until it is very hot. Brush the steaks with a little olive oil and season with salt and pepper. Seal on the griddle and cook to taste, probably about 3–4 minutes on both sides.

Once cooked, brush the steaks with mustard and dip into the herbs. Slice each steak into four to six slices, arrange on a plate and serve with chips and a lemon quarter.

Fillet Steak with Stilton Rarebit

Rarebits are usually associated with toast – and, in one celebrated chef's recipe, with smoked fish – but the combination here of Stilton cheese, beer and beef is great. It's a dish I created at the Hotel du Vin and Bistro; there I served the steak on toast with a liver pâté. This is a simpler version.

SERVES 4

4 x 200g (7oz) fillet steaks

salt and pepper, to taste

3 tbsp olive oil

400ml (14fl oz) red wine

600ml (1 pint) fresh beef stock

approx. 20g (3/4 oz) cold butter, diced

2 tbsp pesto

RAREBIT

2 free-range egg yolks

1 tsp mustard

2 tbsp fresh breadcrumbs

a dash of Worcestershire sauce

a dash of Tabasco sauce

100ml (31/2 fl oz) milk

100ml (31/2 fl oz) beer

115g (4oz) Stilton cheese

Season the fillet steaks well and place in a hot frying pan with the olive oil. Cook on both sides for a total of about 5–6 minutes, then remove from the pan and keep warm. (This gives you a medium steak; if you prefer it cooked more or less than this, cook to the degree you prefer as no further cooking is necessary.)

Keep the pan on full heat and add the wine. Boil to reduce by half, then add the beef stock and continue to reduce.

For the rarebit, place the egg yolks, mustard and breadcrumbs in a bowl along with the Worcestershire and Tabasco sauce. Then stir in the milk and beer, and season well with salt and pepper. Grate the Stilton cheese, and fold in as well. Mix everything together until it has formed a very thick paste.

Preheat the grill to a high heat. Top the steaks with the rarebit and place under the grill until golden brown on the top. Remove from the grill and place on the four plates.

Season the reduced sauce and add the butter to give it a nice glaze. To finish, add the pesto to the sauce, then pour it around the steaks and serve.

Classic Beef Burgers with Soft Onions

Make these burgers with quality mince so you can serve them pink. Prepare them in advance so they can firm up in the fridge before frying. If you plan to barbecue them, seal them in a pan first.

SERVES 4

900g (2lb) best minced beef

salt and pepper, to taste

3 white onions, thinly sliced

30g (1 1/4 oz) unsalted butter

olive oil

TO SERVE

4 burger buns

1 head little gem lettuce, leaves separated

2 medium tomatoes, sliced

Place the meat in a bowl and season. Weigh the meat into 225g (8oz) portions and mould them with your hands into burger shapes. Place the burgers on a tray or plate, cover with clingfilm and leave in the fridge.

When you want to eat the burgers, sauté the onions in a pan in the butter until golden brown, about 10–15 minutes.

Heat a little olive oil in a ridged cast-iron griddle or sauté pan and fry the burgers, depending how you like them. You need 3 minutes each side for medium. Serve the burgers in the buns with a couple of lettuce leaves, some sliced tomato and some soft onion.

Beef Burgers with Bacon
Although beef burgers are usually thought to be American, so many of us have grown up eating them, either from frozen, bought from one of the burger chains or – best of all – homemade, that they have attained British status.

SERVES 4

675g (1 1/2 lb) minced beef

1 tsp French mustard

salt and pepper, to taste

1 shallot, finely diced

1 clove garlic, finely diced

1 tbsp chopped fresh flat-leaf parsley

1 free-range egg

TO COOK AND SERVE

1 tbsp olive oil

25g (1oz) butter

4 rashers bacon

lettuce leaves, shredded

4 burger buns

Combine all of the burger ingredients in a large bowl. Form into four oval-shaped patties.

Sauté the patties in a hot pan in the olive oil and butter for 3–4 minutes on each side. While sautéing, grill the bacon until cooked through.

Place the salad leaves in your bun and put the burger and then bacon on top of the leaves.

Everybody loves burgers, from burnt to a cinder by the old man who once a year takes over the cooking on the barbecue, to the 'drive-thru' eaten from in-between your legs as you drive off to the next meeting. But there's one thing that gets me going, and it's those pretentious chefs who slag off burgers in favour of fillet steak.

The Best Cheeseburger

SERVES 4

2 shallots, chopped

a splash of olive oil

675g (1½ lb) tail of beef fillet

4 tbsp chopped gherkins

2 tbsp double cream

½ tsp Dijon mustard

a splash of Worcestershire sauce

salt and pepper, to taste

1 ball mozzarella cheese, drained and cut into 4 slices

Sauté the chopped shallots quickly in the oil to take off the rawness, then allow to cool.

Mince the fillet of beef into a bowl through the fine plate of a mincer. Add the shallots, gherkins, cream, mustard and Worcestershire sauce. Beat well together and season to taste with salt and pepper.

Using a little oil on your hands, shape the mixture into four even-sized burger shapes. Then, using the palm of your other hand, mould the burger into a bowl shape and place a slice of the mozzarella in the middle. Fold over the meat to enclose it, then reshape into a burger. Leave in the fridge to firm up for at least 30 minutes.

Preheat the grill, then cook the burgers medium-rare, about 4 minutes on each side. Season well.

Kids love to make this recipe as it's great fun to do. It's even better if you can buy a sausage-making machine (they're not too expensive – sometimes under £50). If you can't find one, you can use a piping bag, although it's harder work. Get sausage skins – at least 60cm (2ft) in length – from your local butcher; you can find synthetic ones now as well.

Cumberland Sausage

SERVES 4–6

450g (1lb) boned, skinned shoulder of pork

175g (6oz) hard back pork fat

4 rashers smoked bacon

1 tsp each of grated nutmeg and mace

25g (1oz) white breadcrumbs, soaked in 8 tbsp hot water

salt and pepper, to taste

Cut the pork, fat and bacon into strips, and put first through the coarse blade of a mincing machine, then through the medium blade. Add the spices, then the soaked, squeezed breadcrumbs. Mix well together with your hands, then add salt and plenty of pepper.

Rinse the salt from the sausage skins. Ease one end of a piece of skin on to the cold tap. Run cold water gently through the skin, to make sure there are no splits or large holes. Turn off the tap, remove the skin and ease it on to the long spout of the sausage-making attachment. Screw the whole thing on to the mincing machine with a coarse blade in position.

Feed the pork sausage meat through the mincer again and, as it comes through, slide the skin gently off the attachment and coil it on to a large plate. Leave in the fridge until next day.

When ready to cook, preheat the oven to 180°C/350°F/gas mark 4. Prick the sausage, place on a greased ovenproof tray then bake for 30–45 minutes. Alternatively, fry the coil in a pan on top of the stove, in a little oil – but the oven is easier. The sausage coil is enough for four on its own, or six as part of a meal.

The fact that black pudding is made from pig's blood mixed with oatmeal, suet and onion may not appeal to you, but I consider it one of the best of British tastes (which is good for breakfast as well). Try to buy from good butchers' shops, as black pudding is usually made fresh on the premises. These have much more flavour and taste than the commercial, branded black puddings. I believe black puddings should be sliced and pan-fried. The cooking time is important as well as the heat of the pan, and you don't need much fat. A cooked slice of black pudding should be slightly crisp on the edges but moist in the centre.

Black Pudding with Caramelized Apple and Cider

SERVES 2

1 Golden Delicious apple

55g (2oz) butter

1 tbsp caster sugar

175g (6oz) black pudding, cut into 1cm (1/2 in) slices

50ml (2fl oz) cider

salt and pepper, to taste

Place two frying pans on the stove and heat up to a high heat while you prepare the apple. Core the apple whole, then cut it in half and slice each half into five slices.

Divide the butter between the two pans, and put the sugar in one of them. Place the black pudding into the non-sugared pan, reduce the heat and cook for 2–3 minutes, turning occasionally.

When the sugar and butter in the other pan have started to turn golden brown, add the apple slices. Turn up the heat and quickly caramelize the apple: about 3 minutes. Pour in the cider to deglaze the pan, stirring well, and season quickly with salt and pepper.

To serve, either put the apple mixture and the black pudding into separate bowls or plates for the two of you to help yourselves from, or arrange the black pudding on the two plates with the apple on top.

Corned beef and Spam were the basis of so much food we ate as kids, but they're not deemed trendy any more. Or are they? I cook corned beef hash to remind me of what my auntie used to cook for me. Served with a little salad, it is a satisfying snack that can be eaten at any time of the day. It's good for breakfast, perhaps topped with a fried egg. It can also be made into little patties – when the mix might need to be bound with an egg. In America, corned beef hash is served with Ketchup (*see* page 241) or chilli sauce.

Corned Beef Hash

SERVES 4

2 onions, chopped

1 tbsp fresh thyme leaves

25g (1oz) butter

1 tsp yeast extract

350ml (12fl oz) beef stock

150ml (5fl oz) red wine

375g (13 oz) corned beef

2 tbsp chopped fresh flat-leaf parsley

salt and pepper, to taste

FILLING

250g (9oz) potatoes, peeled

milk, for mashing potatoes

25g (1oz) butter

50g (1 3/4 oz) Cheddar, grated

25g (1oz) fresh breadcrumbs

Preheat the oven to 200°C/400°F/gas mark 6.

For the filling, boil the potatoes in plenty of simmering, salted water. When they are just cooked, remove from the heat and cool in cold water. Drain, dice and leave to one side.

In a large frying pan, fry the onions and thyme in the butter for about 3 minutes. Add the yeast extract, stock and red wine and reduce by half. Add the corned beef, parsley and and some salt and pepper and cook for 5–10 minutes, breaking the beef up with a fork.

Season the cooled potatoes and mash them thoroughly with some milk and the butter.

Place the corned beef mixture into an ovenproof dish and top with the mashed potatoes. Mix the grated cheese together with the breadcrumbs. Sprinkle the mixture over the mashed potatoes and bake for 20 minutes to cook through and brown the top.

Serve with a dressed green salad.

I like calf's liver with onions, but what I really remember is the tripe and onions I had when I was a kid. It's hard to find now. There is one place that still does good tripe and onions, and that's a café in Leeds city centre vegetable market. It tastes great, but what's even better is that the café is full of old blokes telling stories of the old days. A fab place.

Pan-fried Calf's Liver with Bacon and Onions

SERVES 4

8 medium onions, sliced

85g (3oz) butter

8 rashers smoked streaky bacon

100ml (3 1/2 fl oz) Madeira, plus extra for deglazing

900ml (1 1/2 pints) beef or chicken stock

salt and pepper, to taste

675g (1 1/2 lb) calf's liver, thinly sliced

TO SERVE

Mashed Potatoes (*see* page 222)

Preheat the grill to high. Sauté the onions in 25g (1oz) of the butter until well caramelized. This will take about 15 minutes. While the onions are cooking, crisp the bacon under the grill.

Once the onion is ready, add the Madeira and stock and reduce by half, until you have a rich sauce. Check the seasoning and leave to one side.

Heat a frying pan on a high heat and add a knob of the remaining butter. Cook the liver in batches to keep the pan really hot. Season while in the pan. The liver will only take about 1–2 minutes to cook on each side, and should be nice and pink in the middle.

Remove the liver from the pan and deglaze the pan with a little more Madeira, then add the reduced onion sauce as well, and season.

To serve, place the mashed potatoes on the plate, top with the liver and spoon over the sauce. Top with the crispy bacon.

Meatballs with Tomato Sauce

A grown-up version of a kid's delight. I remember hating meatballs as a child, as my nana used to cook them all the time, but they were truly awful, always from a tin and never heated through, and served with a mound of overcooked rice. My sister and I used to be made to sit through this ordeal, and we weren't allowed to leave the table until we had finished. I used to hide mine, anywhere and everywhere I could….But these are infinitely more delicious!

SERVES 4

2 shallots, chopped

1 clove garlic, chopped

olive oil

450g (1lb) tail of beef fillet

2 tsp Dijon mustard

a dash of Worcestershire sauce

50ml (2 fl oz) double cream

salt and pepper, to taste

BASIC TOMATO SAUCE

1.5kg (3lb 5oz) ripe and meaty tomatoes

4 tbsp olive oil

1 medium onion, very finely sliced

1 clove garlic, coarsely chopped

1 tbsp chopped fresh oregano

10 small fresh basil leaves, shredded

For the tomato sauce, plunge the tomatoes into boiling water for 1 minute to loosen the skin. Remove the skin, and cut the tomatoes in half. Discard the inner liquid and seeds. Coarsely chop the remaining flesh.

Heat the oil in a pan and fry the onion for 5 minutes. Add the garlic and fry for a further minute. Add the tomatoes and bring to the boil, then add the oregano, reduce the heat and simmer for 30–40 minutes. Halfway through, add the basil leaves.

When the sauce has finished cooking, add some salt to taste, and liquidize. Keep warm. (The sauce keeps for a few days in the fridge, but is best if eaten when freshly made.)

Meanwhile, to make the meatballs, sauté the shallots and garlic quickly in a little oil to take off the rawness, then allow to cool. Mince the beef through the fine plate of a mincer into a bowl. Add the shallots, garlic, mustard, Worcestershire sauce and cream. Beat well together, then season to taste with salt and pepper.

Using a little oil on your hands, shape the mixture into eight to ten even-sized shapes about the size of a golf ball. Leave for 10 minutes, covered, in the fridge to firm up.

Preheat a pan on the stove and add a little olive oil. Fry the meatballs until golden brown all over, and serve with the warm tomato sauce.

pies & tarts

Masham, which is just off the A1 near Thirsk, has two breweries: Theakstons and the Black Sheep Brewery. It was once also home to one of the largest sheep markets in the country, which was held in the town's market square. That trade has now gone, but the breweries are still going strong. Run by Paul Theakston, the Black Sheep Brewery is open to the public and is well worth a visit. Their strongest beer is Riggwelter; the words 'rigged' and 'welted' in old Yorkshire slang would suggest to a farmer that one of his sheep is upside down. Trust me, a few pints of this stuff, and you'd be rigged too!

Beef and Black Sheep Ale Pie

SERVES 4

900g (2lb) stewing beef, diced

25g (1oz) plain flour

salt and pepper, to taste

butter

2 white onions, sliced

2 cloves garlic, sliced

2 medium carrots, sliced

140g (5oz) button mushrooms, wiped

2 sprigs fresh thyme

1 bay leaf

400ml (14fl oz) Black Sheep Ale

500ml (18fl oz) fresh beef stock

1 free-range egg, beaten, for egg wash

300g (10 1/2 oz) ready-rolled puff pastry

Preheat the oven to 180°C/350°F/gas mark 4, and place a large casserole dish over a medium heat on the stove.

While the dish is heating, place the meat in a bowl, and add the flour and seasoning, turning to coat. When the pan is hot, melt about 15g (1/2 oz) of the butter. Add the meat in batches, adding more butter if necessary, and seal until golden brown all over.

Once browned, add the vegetables, herbs and liquids to the meat and bring to a simmer on the stove. Cover with a lid or some foil, and either gently simmer on top of the stove for 11/2 hours or (what I would do) cook it in the oven for 11/4 hours. Once the meat is tender, season and tip into an ovenproof oven-to-table pie dish. Increase the oven temperature to 200°C/400°F/gas mark 6.

Brush the beaten egg along the edges of the dish and top with the puff pastry. Pinch the edges of the dish so that the pastry will stick to it, and trim off any remaining pieces of pastry from around the edge. Use the pastry trimmings to make leaves, berries and a decorative rope to go along the outside. Make holes in the top for steam to escape. Brush the pastry all over with the remaining egg wash, and place the pie dish on a baking tray.

Bake for 30–40 minutes, until the pastry is golden brown on the top. (Use a baking tray, as the mixture inside the pie dish can sometimes bubble out and make one hell of a mess on the bottom of your cooker.)

Steak and Kidney Pie

Great pub food is one of the joys of where I live, and steak and kidney pie is one of my faves. There are so many variations of this classic. Some say it should have oysters, beer or stout in the mix, but I think this one is the nicest I've cooked. Besides, would you want me to give you a recipe with beef, kidneys and oysters topped with pastry? I don't think so. Although purists say this pie should be made with shortcrust pastry, I feel puff pastry makes a much better topping.

SERVES 4

1 x 300g pack puff pastry

1 free-range egg and 1 extra free-range egg yolk, beaten together

FILLING

25g (1oz) beef dripping or 2 tbsp vegetable oil

700g (1lb 9oz) stewing beef, diced

200g (7oz) lamb's kidney, diced

2 medium onions, diced

8 button mushrooms, halved

25g (1oz) plain flour

1/2 tbsp tomato purée

700ml (1 1/4 pints) beef stock

150ml (5fl oz) red wine

salt and pepper, to taste

2 tbsp chopped fresh parsley

a dash of Worcestershire sauce

Heat the dripping or vegetable oil in a large frying pan, and use to seal the beef in batches until well coloured. Browning the meat is important, as it gives the pie a really deep golden colour.

Brown the kidney in the same pan, then add the onions and mushrooms and cook for 3–4 minutes.

Return all the meat to the pan, then sprinkle the flour over to coat the meat and vegetables. Add the tomato purée, stock and red wine to the pan, stir well and bring to the boil. Turn the heat down and simmer for 1 1/2 hours without a lid on. If the liquid is evaporating too much, add a little more stock.

Shortly before the end of the cooking time, preheat the oven to 220°C/425°F/gas mark 7.

Add some salt and pepper, the parsley and Worcestershire sauce to the filling. Leave to cool slightly.

Place the cooked meat mixture into a pie dish. Roll out the pastry to 5mm (1/4in) thick, and 5cm (2in) larger than the dish you are using. Cut a strip of pastry to fit around the edge of the pie dish, and stick it down using a little water. Brush the top with beaten egg.

Use the rolling pin, lift the pastry and place it over the top of the pie dish. Trim and crimp the edges with your fingers and thumb. Brush all over the surface with the beaten egg and decorate with any pastry trimmings. Brush any decorations with beaten egg. Bake for 30–40 minutes. I love this with either mash, peas or carrots or – to hell with it – have all three!

Cornish Pasty

You can find all sorts of fancy recipes for Cornish pasties, but the simple ones are the best. This dish was never invented to achieve stars in restaurants. It is what it is: a good gut filler (and even better warm, of course). I have kept this recipe very simple and made it here with ready-made pastry, but you can make your own pastry if you wish.

SERVES 2

500g (1lb 2oz) ready-made shortcrust pastry

1 free-range egg, beaten, to glaze

FILLING

250g (9oz) rump steak

115–140g (4–5oz) onions, chopped

85g (3oz) turnip, chopped

225g (8oz) potato, peeled and thinly sliced

salt and pepper, to taste

a pinch of dried thyme

To make the filling, remove the fat from the lean meat, and cut the meat into rough cubes. Mix together with the vegetables, salt, pepper and thyme.

Preheat the oven to 180°C/350°F/gas mark 4.

Roll out the pastry and cut it into two large dinner-plate circles. Divide the steak mixture between the two, putting it down the middle. Brush the rim of the pastry with beaten egg. Fold over the pastry, to make a half circle, or bring up the two sides to meet over the top of the filling, and pinch them together into a scalloped crest going right over the top of the pasty. Make two holes on top, so that the steam can escape.

Place the pasties on a baking sheet and brush them with beaten egg. Bake for 40 minutes. Serve hot or cold.